Where I Live
Some of the Time

poems by

Barry Vitcov

Finishing Line Press
Georgetown, Kentucky

Where I Live
Some of the Time

ACKNOWLEDGMENTS

Where I Live Some of the Time: *EAP: The Magazine,* Spring 2019
A Contortionist Writing an Extemporaneous Poem: *EAP: The Magazine,*
    Summer 2019
My 70-Year Old Bucket List (Amended): *EAP: The Magazine,* Fall 2019
Portraits of Angels in the Sky: *EAP: The Magazine,* Winter 2019
Billy's Bee: EAP: The Magazine, Spring 2019
Desdemona's Corpse: *Literary Yard,* September 7, 2019
Gefilte Fish: *Literary Yard,* September 7, 2019
Spider Web Tango: *Literary Yard,* September 7, 2019
There's a Pet Crate: *Literary Yard,* September 7, 2019
Her Beauty Was Not an Open Lie: *Scarlet Leaf Review,* January 2020
Deconstruction: *Scarlet Leaf Review,* January 2020
Gefilte Fish: *Vita Brevis,* November 22, 2019
We Stood Together at the Shore: *The Drabble,* November 22, 2019

Publisher: Leah Huete de Maines
Editor: Christen Kincaid
Cover Art: William E. Saltzstein
Author Photo: William E. Saltzstein
Cover Design: Elizabeth Maines McCleavy

Order online: www.finishinglinepress.com
        also available on amazon.com

Author inquiries and mail orders:
Finishing Line Press
P. O. Box 1626
Georgetown, Kentucky 40324
U. S. A.

Table of Contents

Perspectives

Travels

Poodles

Villanelles

For Shirley

and all those who have supported and encouraged me...

thank you!

Perspectives

Where I Live Some of the Time

The night sky is my home
Its emptiness tucked between supernovas and black holes
Welcoming me into imagined places

I'm pedaling my space bike
A modified road trike
Across the universe

Counting handfuls of stars
Fluffy cotton candy bars
Woven into fanciful shapes

When a mermaid catches my eye
Like an interstellar spy
Beckoning me with a fishtail wiggle

I raise my eyebrows in disbelief
Feeling a sense of cosmic relief
Suppressing a whisper of a giggle

Who cares to understand eternity
When wrapped in the easiness of
Cosmic subtlety

Desdemona's Corpse

Desdemona is asked how to play a corpse
Shallow breaths
Running future lines in my head
She said

When confined to bed
And my cells are almost done
No longer subject to the sun
When roses no longer bloom
Nor sweeten the air with their perfume
My room forever empty
My breath growing shallow

I'll run dreams in my head
With pictures for you to imagine

When we walked in a park
For the first time
Became intoxicated when smelling peonies
Drank coffee with endless abandon
Spoke of the future
Lived in the present
Wistfully measured the distance between the two
Looked at each other for the first time every day in those early years
Found the power of quiet touch
Made love outdoors by the creek

Those are the dreams
I'll leave for you

Desdemona's corpse is alive
And so is mine

My 70-year Old Bucket List (Amended)

This 70-year old Jew
Wants a slew of pork belly
Crispy and succulent
I want meat from
Rabbits and ostriches
No brisket, kishkes, or latkes will do

I want a threesome of
Clams, oysters, and lobsters
Sucking out sweet, chewy flesh
Even in a fishy, frothy stew of
Shrimp and other bottom filters
Will certainly do

I want a ham and Swiss
On lily-white bread
Slathered with Hellman's mayonnaise and Beaver's Sweet Hot mustard
With a goyishe beer like Adolf Coors
And salty Philadelphia pretzels
Reminding me of youth
Although a Budweiser pony size will do

I want the best dill pickle money can buy
Snap crisp and garlicy
A small bucket of vinegary giardiniera
Several bleu cheeses
Chopped liver and other dietary challenges

I want a fully restored 1955 Ford Thunderbird
Goldenrod yellow exterior and black interior
Built years before I was licensed to drive
But I can drive now, baby!
With a picnic basket in the back
And a fast woman sitting in the bucket seat beside me
Driving along the Pacific
With only fantasies on my mind

Old Friend Calls

No ocean view from this sprawling Carmel house
Above the village and below the highway
Situated like a bride's maid
Waiting for another's adventures to begin
Surrounded by art and randomness
A confused clutter of lived-in-ness
The security of electronic possessions
Telling a lonely story
While ceramic geese virtually honk
At an artificial fireplace

And the phone rings
A friend saying her brother just died
It wasn't unexpected
But fit with an unprotected moment
Like most moments
Predictive surprise

Gefilte Fish

There are always a couple of jars of gefilte fish in the fridge
And a couple of back-up jars in the cupboard
I must alert my wife before opening one
She can't tolerate the smell
And the plate I use must be thoroughly rinsed
Before being placed in the dishwasher
I don't think it's about the plate holding kosher food
Contaminating the other Christian dishes
At least I hope not

It seems that my son has inherited a distaste for this delicacy
He snickers when I have a couple smothered in horseradish
I prefer the red beet colored horseradish over the white prepared variety
With a couple of dry matzos on the side
(Which he enjoys with butter and jelly)
But his Chinese girlfriend enthusiastically tried some
Savoring it for some time
Before declaring it good
I think our cultures have quite a bit in common

I used to eat at a Chinese Muslim restaurant
The food was halal and close enough to kosher
I've never kept kosher but enjoy the experience
I'm not a believer in myths
I rather cherish the secular results
And Moses is the most mentioned prophet in the Quran
Unfortunately Abraham's choices cleaved two cultures
Families are strange sometimes

Spider Web Tango

The fragility of spider webs is age-related
Astonishing old timers
Whose web-making becomes more chaotic
Over time and decomposition

These intricate structures
Composed like Brazilian tangos
With rhythms and sensual undertones
Seductive entrapments
Growing ancient and intertwined

Spider webs collapse from the weight of dust
And their remains are used to build another
The residue of toil transferred
Like mass and energy
The physics of our lives

Tapestry

Centuries of foot traffic
Worn into an ancient carpet
An intricate design
Of every hue and thread
Between eastern and western seas
Northern and southern continents
The middle pulling apart
Filaments torn by grief and despair
Edges struggling for a share
As the center is eviscerated
Like wolves devouring their corpse
While Turkey Vultures circle for carrion

Where are the weavers
Repairers of old myths
Working with fine needles
Combs, scissors, hooked knives, and brushes
Who might stitch together shared values
While finding future beliefs
Common enough to resist tyranny
The whims and fancies of ignorance
Peaks of fevered debates
Valleys of shared tranquility
Mending a strengthened tapestry

Takamine Guitar Love Song

Came upon an old
Mottled Takamine six-string guitar
Hovering in a ditch along Hwy 99
Wagging its fret board
Like a Salvador Dali witch's finger
Simultaneously inviting and chastising
The mother of every lover
In a western melodrama

Beckoning with acoustic love songs
For anyone caring to listen
Under a turpentine sky
February is a month to cry
For one lost
Another found
Romantic tunes
Just blues by another sound

My Smart Phone

My smart phone is really smart
Touched it and a genie appeared
Poof! A holographic app
All green and blue
Smiling too like a venomous dart
A bit too toothy if you ask me
A wavering nuclear cloud
Inquiring aloud
What would you command me to do
At first I thought it was a hoax
An accumulation of hallucinogenic jokes
I asked the turbaned figure for a moment
Wondering what step to take next
The enigma replied in a melodious text
Make it a wise choice
One wish only
Use a strong persuasive voice
Think about the consequences
Technology isn't science
Just a dream of immortality

Ransom Note Poetry

Snipping words and images from magazines
Catalogs, political pamphlets, garage sale flyers
Discarded novels rarely read
A short story or two
You alone
Sipping chamomile tea
Me…a refugee… from a lesser known café
Writing ransom note poetry
To unmet lovers
Arranging scraps of my life
Sorting experiences into piles
For later use

Staring into cappuccino foam
A barista artist's hearts
Slowly absorbed
I paste roses, tulips, lilacs
A comical arrangement
On a blank page
Feel you sit beside me
Dip your finger into my coffee
Trace an ellipse
In the palm of my hand
And smile
An address for a poem

New Year Japanese Maple

Winter teases
Like an impressionable child
Snow rimed Japanese maple
The skeleton of lighted reindeer
Emitting an inner glow
On a virgin white lawn
Ice crystals appearing
As blooms of the season's memory
Kept in a frozen jar
North star
Dominant in an uncluttered sky
Inhale the tapestry of the New Year

Pausing to Savor the Wind

Pausing to savor the wind
Sifting through reeds
Like an atonal alto sax
Chilling my ears and fears
With omens of rain, sleet, snow, and freeze
Listening to fall welcoming winter
Last leaves slipping and sidling down the block
Sounds of shivering maracas
Deer sniffing the air
With the attitude of an aristocrat
Squirrels working overtime
What we hear we cannot see
Imagining a musical interlude
Bridging the season's first falling snowflakes
Piling like a knitted muffler
Feeling cool tears of rejuvenation

Semicolons and Politicians

I've been thinking a lot about the semicolon
Not about its colon cousin
That's another poem in waiting
And the apostrophe has an entire society
Dedicated to its preservation
Can you imagine?

It's the semicolon
That dot with a wink intending to join together
Closely related, yet
Independent clauses
A sweet notion: bringing together independence
Of course, that last line called for a colon

A colon, after all, can be a powerful piece of punctuation
Except when used by politicians
Who simply want to burden us with loud lists
Finger pointing punctuation bliss
Turning bullet points into twitter tweets
Used when deeper thinking is absent and listing is easy:
Distresses, redresses,
Professed priorities, demonstrations of rote knowledge,
Grievances, all-inclusive likes and dislikes
Concerns without a discerning point of view

On the other hand, semicolons are like progressives
Nuanced and mature
Not oral diarrhea; rather, closely constructed statements
Semicolons bridge thinking; create insights
Describing a presence; offering a future
No shallow highlights here
Reflection takes time and good punctuation

Counting Florets After an Election

I keep trying to count the florets
Woven into my Persian carpet
A handmade Iranian masterpiece
Bought for several thousand dollars
Made for a few hundred
Shades and shapes repeated
Rosettes, tulips, starbursts
Burgundies, carmines, purples
A variety of intertwined life

Florets form curious patterns
A coherence in constant flux
Pushing and stretching imaginations
Like sci-fi cinema with hope
Dread, determination, tender fingers
Pulling yarn through impassable places
Pictures emerging as the tapestry unfolds

Design choices expressing a point of view
Made temporary by wear and tear
Whatever the rug can bear
Some florets more lasting than others
An imperfect mystery unraveled over time
Its lasting value measured
Not by its perfections
But by its persistence

Red Cat Writes a Poem

A red cat
Tensed before a gopher hole
Focused attention and intention
Eyes like needles
Claws extended in c-shaped shivs
While I try writing a poem
Too many random metaphors
Like hummingbirds choosing one blossom over another

That cat doesn't move
Barely quivers
Finds solace in concentration
There must be a better way
Spending my rhyme
Wondering about life and love
The end of time
Existential authors
Circumstances flipped like flapjacks
Ready when the sap runs

That cat's stillness interrupted
A slick nose flutters
A paw strikes forward
Misses
Angry hisses
Intensity resumed
My eyes catch leaves falling
Tangerine, withering, covering
That gopher hole

As leaves pile
One matching leaf after another
Perfectly stacked
Edges aligned
That cat relaxes and saunters by
Crisp air and equilibrium

A Contortionist Writing an Extemporaneous Poem

A contortionist writing an extemporaneous poem
Shaping herself into words
One letter at a time
Alone
Giving more to the word
Than what was intended
With flourishes of twists and turns
Not unlike a white-faced mime
A body morphed into letters
Lose their humankind
Unable to distinguish fonts, bold and sublime

Some letters are easily flexed
Others painful G's and B's
Twisting a poem leaves no impression
Like the scent of roses
The wisp of fog
The rhythm of seas
Flashy serifs
Meant to embellish
The bland shape of calligraphy

A contortionist writing an extemporaneous poem
Erasing itself as each letter is formed
Undoing each shape as the next one is born
A poem leaves no impression
Only its form

Blackberries

Watching a group of teens
Strutting down the block
With pride, purpose and stained smiles
Swinging pails of freshly-picked blackberries
Hands and lips smeared blackish blue
Youth dripping from their chins
Watcha gonna do with that fruit
I ask
Make some pies
They chorus
Done it before
I ask
Nope
First time for everything
I close my eyes and dream

Grandfather Built This House

Grandfather built this house
Foundation to weathervane
Hand trimmed winter bougainvillea canes
Shaggy and resolute
Like my monthly haircut
While seated on a stool
In his garage surrounded
By woodworking tools
And dill pickles
Salty and garlicky
Prepared by my bubbe
Neighbors called him a community kook
For hand auguring a well
Till free water made his garden grow
Cucumbers, peas, beans, tomatoes
Filled a five-gallon jug with unpitted cherries
Bags of sugar
A dark closet
Tasting sweet vishnick
With Mandelbrot

Sousa the March King

March arrived in late February
Snow softly tiptoeing like a sleepy housecat
The wind roaring like lions
Seasons changing
Without military precision or derision
Like a discordant band disturbing the end of winter

The poodles and I hunkered down
With books, movies, and occasional treats
Although the puppy found the snow interesting
Especially when pushing icy crystals around with her nose
And running laps in the backyard
The older dog finding the soft, warm confines of her wire crate
More to her liking

While Sousa required the structure of marches
The order of finely-tuned music
The punctuation of drums and fifes
To usher in parades and other public spectacles
I embrace the quirkiness
Of a season's unexpected comedy
I enjoy the anomalies of a good winter storm
And arrhythmic weather
I want to embrace the uncertainty and the burden
Of cyclical change and expectation
Surprise me with a snowball on the Fourth of July

Deconstruction

Deconstructed tacos
They're all the rage
A dollop of carnitas
Or carne asada
Pico de gallo
Arranged artistically on a plain plate
With some corn tortillas
Off to the side
The diner is expected to do the work
Putting the ingredients together
Making a tasty dish
I like it when the drip flowing down my chin
Is just right

And then there are deconstructed stories
With invented language
And punctuation eschewed
No vital cues
Served up as literature
Where the reader is expected to do the work
And make sense of the author's laziness
For goodness sakes
It's already hard enough
Getting inside a writer's head
Not the stories I want to take to bed

I like deconstructed paintings
With their scribbles and lots of white space
A few lines and dots
Arranged on a canvas
Titled nude on a park bench
Invitations to draw my own pictures
Having no ability to draw at all
I imagine nakedness on the wall
My imagined art indistinguishable
From Rubens or Chagall

We Stood Together at the Shore

We stood together at the shore
Watching a pod of dolphins arc
Fondly opening memory's door

Kept just beyond our common reach
The beach warming our bare feet
The gusting air cool and sweet

We review our lives
Pages of diaries filled with truths and lies
Far too often hellos and goodbyes

Our profiles have aged
We look at each other with older eyes
Our love still filled with loving whys

We find ourselves in the ocean's view
I knew you better
When I didn't know you

Billy's Bee

My friend Billy carried a honeybee
Around in a Diamond matchbox
We were five or six or seven
(Specific memories aren't as important as the sense of things)
Tramping around the rocky hill behind our South San Francisco house
It seemed like Mt. Everest at the time
(Still does from time to time)
Every so often he'd slide open the matchbox
The honeybee would tentatively look out
Before flying off
Just a few feet away
Before returning
Billy would slide the box shut
Returning the box to his shirt's breast pocket
Maybe the honeybee felt comfort from Billy's heartbeat

When one bee died
He simply shook it out
And found another to train
I have no idea how he found obedient bees
He never named them
Billy's family eventually moved away
I never met another bee trainer

We live in boxes
Not much of a life to share
Go from here to there

We live in boxes
built by our own creation
imagined or not

Travels

Zion

Walking through Zion Canyon
Mauve, gray, rust and other oxidic rock
Mountain goats stepping easily on sedimentary ledges
Not meant for me

Walls waiting like a bride's maid
The Virgin River's testament to history
And of no importance to flora and fauna
Who witness continuous erosion and growth
While composing habits and rhythms
In harmony with their place

I hike along arid trails
Observing what I label significant
Taking pictures like a stalker
Watching water percolate
In silt around a single cottonwood
A moment in nature's composition
While my own composition
Is decomposition

Monterey Pines Framing Carmel Beach

Monterey pines framing Carmel beach
Like a lover's fragrant hands
A cello's bow pulling the rhythm of tides
Washing away thoughts I might have had
While watching gray squirrels
Tense at my intrusion

What is it about rodents
Seemingly without conscience
Constantly at work
Scrounging for food
Oblivious to the consequences of their actions

Or is it my jealous rage
An inability to accept these dismal creatures
For what they are
One of nature's sight gags

Road Hard

Aspens jingle like loose change
God painted a cloud
That could not rain
An Australian cattle dog curls up
Looks once in my direction
Goes to sleep

Breezes cool the summer sun
A large ant appears lost on a stone
A radio tower two miles away
Maintains conversations
Civilized and uncivilized

At camp there's a tent
Through its roof infinite stars
A pine burned fifty feet away
Concern ourselves with today

Pop Agie River, Wyoming

Pop Agie whitewater
Like lovers in heat
Its edges moving calmly
Smooth as a silk sheet
At center, the fastest water,
A deliciously shuddering beat

As the sun settles on Sinks Canyon
White, translucent moths appear
Somewhere in its granite cliffs
A lover's echo moans
And deer drink from still pools
Beavers work their ponds
Hands intertwine

Woman Climber

Pulling up a cliff
Feet glued to the limestone
Like dimes on an oil slick
Her body moving forcefully
Fingers searching for elusive holds
When she falls
A mild cry escapes her lips
Like a lover's sigh
The rock is soft
And the climb begins again
Holding the rope in her teeth
Nudging it into a carabiner
Dark-haired beauty slender and
Long
Muscled
Loves stone

Sitting at the Bread Story Bakery

Surrounded by cats
Almost as extreme as Istanbul
What is it about Mediterranean's
And feline creatures
Is it the Lion of Judah
Linking every Israeli soul
Like a keeper of fierceness
Preserving a culture
Forever under siege

Cats are acrobatic
Like dancing waves of light
Prismatic and comedic
Enduring and escaping
Darkness with an illusionist's
Sleight of hand
Landing with confidence on their homeland
Much like Israelis

Sitting Inside the Jaffa Gate

Inside the Jaffa Gate
Streaming with uncounted cultures
And I'm sitting at a table
Eating a wonderful falafel
Surrounded by French tourists
One looks to be a priest
But no one seems particularly reverent
For example
They won't engage me in English
For crying out loud
The entire world speaks English
Over here
Well, all but the French
Where the hell is Mark Twain
When I need him

What!
I stand, ready to walk away
I hear one say we are Russian
Now really!
Russians impersonating the French

Sitting in the Synagogue at Yad Vashem

What becomes of lost souls
Whether believers or not
Who enter the void
Without their permission
Torn from their humanity
Made naked
Like all lives
Beginning to end

I am not one for prayer
But I pray for these lives
Who must be of the blessed
For whom we must all bear
Future responsibility

Small Brown Bird in Israel

Small brown bird
Clings effortlessly to a welcome sign
With street clutter chattering below
Its beak pointing and pivoting relentlessly
Its eyes a beat behind
Tail feathers aquiver
Always alert

Tel Aviv's sidewalks filled
Pedestrians, dog-walkers, cyclists, electric scooters
Zig-zagging without collision
Like pinballs with a purpose

That little brown bird
Knows the most opportune
Time to dive for a crumb

Rothschild Blvd.

Unending traffic
Alongside this leafy promenade
A cool shadow of relief
Pedestrians on one side
Cyclists on the other
There is no zig-zagging here
Unusual order for Tel Aviv
Where speed and modernity
Demand their space

Google and Waze
Everyone is global positioning
It's a barn dance on Rothschild Boulevard
Swing your partner to the right
Dosey doe another night
Technology is a distracting sight
For the Bauhaus mansions

Poodles

Poodle Walks

Every day I take the same walk
Along the same sidewalks
Smudged by deer and dog shit
Up the same hill
To a nearby neighborhood
Where the average age increases
In proportion to the slope of the hill climbed

I'm with my poodles
Black on the left; white on the right
The white with a month's life left
We trudge along and I hope
For no distractions causing the dogs
To get out of sync
Their paws and my feet in a pleasant melody
Of course the old people point and smile

The routine is expected
When I ask do you want to go for a walk
Enthusiasm is high; harnesses and leashes welcomed
Poodles never seem to notice
The changes I observe
Empty houses where seniors once lived
Or their own mortality

Hummingbird and Poodle

Hummingbird hovering at coral lilies
My poodle fascinated
Still head and fixated black eyes
Silent prey without a real threat
While the ocean tolls background music
Some try to find connections
With these curiosities
But poetry is not physics
And mathematics is often random

There's a Pet Crate

There's a pet crate in the middle of my living room
Where my standard poodles often lounge
We call it a condominium
I doubt they discern any difference
Between a wire crate and luxury living
Although the crate has a fluffy pad on its floor
And does rest on a carpet
An inexpensive carpet
But a carpet no less

One black and one white poodle
They won't share their open-air condo
It's always one dog at a time
They seem possessive of their space
I often wonder if dogs are connivers
Seekers of the unknown and misunderstood

I'm always apologizing to the UPS and FedEx
Deliverers because of my dogs' harsh barking
There doesn't even need to be a package left at our door
Just the sound of the vans idling outside initiates
A barrage of guttural barks and yelps
I seem to be the only one disturbed by impulsive mayhem
Disguised as affection

Villanelles

Her Beauty Was Not an Open Lie

Her beauty was not an open lie
Regardless of what others had to say
It hurt too much to say goodbye

Whispers like corrosive alkali
Causing discord and hurtful feelings
Her beauty was not an open lie

What might we do, you and I
Resistance is a hard veil to build
It hurt too much to say goodbye

While others scheme and mystify
I find comfort in your soft embrace
Her beauty was not an open lie

Listen to a wistful tune and cry
Our love was soon becoming lost
It hurt too much to say goodbye

We found ourselves in mid-sigh
In a park beneath an unburdened sky
Her beauty was not an open lie
It hurt too much to say goodbye

That's Our Boy

Your real pleasure is your envy
While others sigh and look away
What you are you cannot see

What you want you cannot be
The greatest leader among leaders
Your real pleasure is your envy

Your heart and thoughts are empty
Like a pig sty without a boar or sow
What you are you cannot see

Lacking care, respect and empathy
Cheered by hateful folks of your ilk
Your real pleasure is your envy

Temperament impedes intellectuality
A rambling and bumbling buffoon
What you are you cannot see

Narcissism is your necessity
Success unattainable ultimately
Your real pleasure is your envy
What you are you cannot see

Portraits of Angels in the Sky

Portraits of angels in the sky
Portraits imagined on a day
Disguised as clouds floating high

Painting pictures of times gone by
Painting images in blues and grays
Portraits of angels in the sky

Whimsical shapes morphing nigh
Dancing in shadowy arrays
Disguised as clouds floating high

Sketching ideas without a why
Depicting others in their own ways
Portraits of angels in the sky

Wayward forms that often belie
Their natures that freely play
Disguised as clouds floating high

Visions of futures we might surmise
Alive without death or decay
Portraits of angels in the sky
Disguised as clouds floating high

The Remains from this Theft

The remains from this theft
Simmering in a dark heart
With the love we have left

Lives sometimes lost and deaf
Lives not lived so smart
The remains from this theft

Relationships rendered bereft
Like viscera torn apart
With the love we have left

With all that we can heft
Pushing uphill a heavy cart
The remains from this theft

Emotions voiced with great depth
Actors skillfully play the part
With the love we have left

What begins as romance with deft
Becomes a choice at the start
The remains from this theft
With the love we have left

We Kept Our Secrets Locked Away

We kept our secrets locked away
In a lonely warming heart
For stories told another day

Thoughts and feelings led astray
An unbalanced one-wheeled cart
We kept our secrets locked away

There was little more we had to say
At the time we had to part
For stories told another day

When fond memories began to fade
As some stars do from a chart
We kept our secrets locked away

And then we found another way
To sweeten a life gone tart
For stories told another day

Searching for a new precious start
Where truths could not keep us apart
We kept our secrets locked away
For stories told another day

We Stood Alone at the Water's Edge

We stood alone at the water's edge
Surveying the vastness that lay ahead
Imagining the perils beyond the ledge

Each one of us had taken a solemn pledge
Regardless of the politics shared and read
We stood alone at the water's edge

The importance of all we might allege
Depends upon the truths and lies we've been fed
Imagining the perils beyond the ledge

Words and actions have driven a wedge
Dividing a nation that's often mislead
We stood alone at the water's edge

Like a clogged channel needing to be dredged
Searching for answers in a deep, murky bed
Imagining the perils beyond the ledge

We are kept from moving through the sedge
And finding tranquility in our heads
We stood alone at the water's edge
Imagining the perils beyond the ledge

Barry Vitcov is a retired educator having spent 45 years as a middle school English teacher, school administrator, leadership coach, and adjunct university professor. He lives in Ashland, Oregon with his wife and two standard poodles. As a teenager, he fondly remembers his father carrying a small collection of his poems in his billfold and showing them off to friends and customers. Barry was raised in the San Francisco Bay Area where he was privileged to experience the 1960's energy, diversity and music as a high school and college student. While attending San Fernando Valley State College (now California State University, Northridge), he was mentored by Newdigate Prize winning poet David Posner and professor and poet Benjamin Saltman. During his educational career, he wrote very little fiction and poetry, as he was immersed in his work. After retirement, he began writing again and continues to hone his literary voice. He has had fiction and poetry published in *EAP: The Magazine, Literary Yard, Scarlet Leaf Review, Vita Brevis, Finding the Birds,* and *The Drabble.*